DEUTERONOMY

The Lord Your God

Bryson Smith

CROSSWAY BOOKS • WHEATON, ILLINOIS
A DIVISION OF GOOD NEWS PUBLISHERS

Deuteronomy: The Lord Your God

First U. S. edition published 1999 by Crossway Books
a division of Good News Publishers
1300 Crescent Street
Wheaton, Illinois 60187

First published 1997 in Australia by Matthias Media under the title *The One and Only.*

Cover design: David LaPlaca

Cover photo: © Dennis Flaherty Photography

Printed in the United States of America

ISBN 1-58134-093-1

---

15 14 13 12 11 10 09 08 07 06 05 04 03 02 01 00 99
15 14 13 12 11 10 9 8 7 6 5 4 3 2 1

Contents

How to Make the Most of These Studies

1. What Is an Interactive Bible Study?

These "interactive" Bible studies are a bit like a guided tour of a famous city. The studies will take you through Deuteronomy, pointing out things along the way, filling in background details, and suggesting avenues for further exploration. But there is also time for you to do some sightseeing of your own—to wander off, have a good look for yourself, and form your own conclusions.

In other words, we have designed these studies to fall halfway between a sermon and a set of unadorned Bible study questions. We want to provide input and point you in the right direction, while leaving you to do a lot of the exploration and discovery yourself.

We hope that these studies will stimulate lots of interaction—interaction with the Bible, with the things we've written, with your own current thoughts and attitudes, with other people as you study with them, and with God as you talk to Him about it all.

2. The Format

Each study focuses on a particular passage or group of passages and contains sections of text to introduce, summarize, suggest, and provoke. Interspersed throughout the text are two types of "interaction," each with its own symbol:

FINDING TRUTH

Questions to help you investigate key parts of the Bible.

GOING FURTHER

Questions to help you think through the implications of your discoveries.

When you come to one of these symbols, you'll know that it's time to do some work on your own.

3. Suggestions for Individual Study

- Before you begin, pray that God would open your eyes to what He is saying in Deuteronomy and give you the spiritual strength to do something about it. You may be spurred to pray again at the end of the study.
- Work through the study, following the directions as you go. Write in the spaces provided.
- Resist the temptation to skip over the *Finding Truth* and *Going Further* sections. It is important to think about the sections of text (rather than just accepting them as true) and to ponder the implications for your life. Writing these things down is a valuable way to get your thoughts working.
- Take what opportunities you can to talk to others about what you've learned.

4. Suggestions for Group Study

- Much of what we have suggested above applies to group study as well. The studies are suitable for structured Bible study or cell groups, as well as for more informal pairs and threesomes. Get together with one or more friends and work on the studies at your own pace. You don't need the formal structure of a "group" to gain maximum benefit.
- It is vital that group members work through the study themselves *before* the group meets. The group discussion can take place comfortably in an hour (depending on how sidetracked

you get!), but only if all the members have done the work and are familiar with the material.

- Spend most of the group time discussing the "interactive" sections—*Finding Truth* and *Going Further*. Reading all the text together would take too long and should be unnecessary if the group members have done their preparation. You may wish to underline and read aloud particular paragraphs or sections of text that you think are important.

- The role of the group leader is to direct the course of the discussion and try to draw the threads together at the end. This will mean a little extra preparation—underlining important sections of text to emphasize, deciding which questions are worth concentrating on, being sure of the main thrust of the study. Leaders will also probably want to decide approximately how long they'd like to spend on each part.

- We haven't included an "answer guide" to the questions in the studies. This is a deliberate move. We want to give you a guided tour of Deuteronomy, not a lecture. There is enough material in the studies to point you in what we think is the right direction. The rest is up to you.

1

What's This About Birds' Nests?

"Make tassels on the four corners of the cloak you wear."
"Do not muzzle an ox while it is treading out the grain."
"If you come across a bird's nest beside the road . . ."

For a lot of people, the book of Deuteronomy, like much of the Old Testament, is daunting. We start to read it with all good intentions but abandon the task a quarter of the way in, because it's just so long! To make things worse, there are certain parts of Deuteronomy that just don't seem to make sense. In chapter 22 we find instructions about what to do if we find a bird's nest by the road. A couple of verses later we are given some Jewish fashion tips on cloak making. We start to wonder why we are reading Deuteronomy at all. We are hard pressed to see how these ancient commands given through Moses can be of any relevance to us.

These studies will help us see how and why Deuteronomy is important for Christians. When we boil it down, Deuteronomy is about *our* God. As we read Deuteronomy we're reading about how *our* God does things. We're reading about how people ought to be responding to our God.

Certainly, there are some differences between twentieth-century Christians and the Israelites led by Moses. But as we'll see, there are also a lot of similarities. The biggest similarity is that both we and Israel are dealing with the same Creator of the universe. God Himself is the common link between Deuteronomy and us. The God of Deuteronomy is the same God to whom we pray.

We can't afford to have merely a polite, historical curiosity about what's in Deuteronomy. Deuteronomy is God's word to us. If you are a Christian, Deuteronomy is part of your heritage as one of God's people. As we start our journey through Deuteronomy, we can expect that the God of Moses and Israel will reveal things about Himself and about us that will shake us to the core!

Let's jump straight into chapter 1.

FINDING TRUTH

Read Deuteronomy 1:1-8.

1. *Where* is the action taking place? Find the location on an Old Testament map. Jordan in the wilderness in the plain over against the Red Sea, between Paran, and Tophel, Laban, and Hazeroth, and Diza hab.
2. How long *should* it take to travel from Horeb to the edge of Kadesh Barnea? Find these places on a map and note the distance.

3. How long *has* it taken Israel to get here? (v. 3)

Late for a Date

The first three verses of Deuteronomy 1 set the scene for most of the book. Verses 2-3 tell us that Israel has taken more than 40 years to travel what could have taken 11 days. Israel is 39 years, 354 days late in getting to the Promised Land! Obviously, something terrible has happened.

So what went wrong? Did Moses have the map upside down? Did they hit all the red lights? Were they just slow walkers? How on earth could Israel take so long?

The short answer is that Israel had messed up a previous attempt to enter Canaan. Moses reminds them of this in the rest of the chapter.

FINDING TRUTH

Read Deuteronomy 1:19-40.
In your own words summarize what happened the last time Israel tried to enter the Promised Land. What made God angry?

Keeping Old Promises

As we've now discovered, Deuteronomy opens with Israel poised on the eastern side of the Jordan River. In other words, they are standing on the edge of what was called "the Promised Land." This description dates back to an ancient promise. This was a region that God had promised to give to Abraham's descendants way back in Genesis 12.

Genesis 12 is a very important chapter of the Old Testament. (If you're not familiar with this chapter, it might be good to turn back now and read Genesis 12:1-9.) Genesis 12 is set at a time when sin was running out of control. The world had been created good (Gen. 1), but ever since the Fall, when Adam and Eve rebelled against God (Gen. 2–3), the world had degenerated into a squalid wasteland of murder, sexual immorality, conspiracy, and deceit. Indeed, things were *such* a mess that God would have been quite justified simply to wipe everyone out and start all over again (this almost happened in Genesis 6–9).

But in Genesis 12, God appears to Abraham (called Abram in that chapter) and very generously promises three things that, rather than heralding destruction, will help restore God's friendship with mankind. God promises that:

i) Abraham will have many descendants,

ii) they will be blessed, and

iii) they will have their own land, stretching up the eastern edge of the Mediterranean Sea.

Over time, God begins to fulfil these promises. Abraham's descendants *do* start to increase. In fact, they grow so numerous that the Egyptians become afraid of them and put them into slavery (Ex. 1). But God keeps His promise to bless Israel and, under Moses' leadership, God rescues them in a blaze of miracles in the Exodus. God parts the Red Sea and leads them out of Egypt, gathering them together at Horeb (also called Mt. Sinai). At Horeb, God speaks to Israel and then leads them out toward the Promised Land.

As we open the book of Deuteronomy, we find all of Abraham's descendants on the edge of that Promised Land. But they have been here once before. They reached the outskirts of the Promised Land fairly quickly after receiving God's commandments at Mt. Sinai. But they failed to trust God and refused to enter the Promised Land (Deut. 1:26-33). As a punishment, God turned them around and made them wander in the wilderness for forty years (vv. 34-40).

Just as you might send a disobedient child to his or her room, God sent a disobedient Israel into the desert to think over their "attitude problem." But now it's time to open the door and come out. The time of discipline has ended. The forty years are over, and Israel is back at the borders of Canaan, ready to receive the fulfillment of God's promise to Abraham.

GOING FURTHER

1. Imagine you are one of the Israelites standing on the edge of the Promised Land in Deuteronomy 1:1. What are your hopes and fears for the future?

2. From a single nomad, Abraham, God has brought forth a nation. He has miraculously rescued them from the super-power, Egypt. Then He left Israel wandering in the desert for forty years because of their disobedience.

   What have you learned about the character of our God from Deuteronomy 1?

Read 1 Corinthians 10:1-13.

3. What should we learn from God's punishment of Israel in the desert?

4. Why does God discipline us?

5. Are these hard instructions to obey? How can we help each other obey them?

Three Talks

With Israel standing on the edge of the Jordan River and looking across to the destination they have taken so long to reach, Moses "proclaimed to the Israelites all that the LORD had commanded him concerning them" (v. 3).

Verse 3 pretty well summarizes what Deuteronomy is all about. It isn't a collection of strange commandments about birds' nests and tassels. The book is a collection of three talks Moses gave to Israel just before they tried for the second time to enter the Promised Land. In all three sermons, Moses passes on God's instructions in order to make sure that Israel has learned from her previous mistakes. We also have much to learn from Israel's mistakes.

Know Whom You're Dealing With

This study looks at Moses' first (and shortest) sermon to Israel. Remember the setting of Deuteronomy from study 1: Israel is about to make another effort to enter the Promised Land. They messed up their first effort because of disobedience, and consequently they spent forty years wandering in the wilderness as punishment. Throughout Deuteronomy, Moses preaches three sermons to make sure that they behave properly this time.

GOING FURTHER

Imagine you are Moses addressing the people. What would you be concerned about? What are some of the things you would say?

In this first sermon, Moses spends a lot of time reminding Israel of what has been happening during their years in the wilderness. He does this because he wants to highlight what God is like. He wants to remind Israel about the way God does things, so that they will understand whom it is they are dealing with.

The sermon begins at Deuteronomy 1:5. Moses recalls how Israel grumbled rebelliously against God's command to enter the Promised Land. They refused to trust that God would let them conquer Canaan's tough inhabitants. Despite the fact that God had kept them safe through thick and thin, they would not trust Him. In anger, God vowed not to let this generation enter the land. They spent the next forty years wandering, but God did not abandon them during this time. Instead, He strengthened them so that, after the period of discipline, they could receive the land of their inheritance.

Deuteronomy 1–3 describes a God who is not afraid to get involved with the world. It describes a God who is big, but who is also personal. God is prepared to be intimately involved in people's lives. He interacts with His people. He talks to His people. He loves His people.

This isn't a God who is a long way off in the distance, standing with His arms folded on the sideline. This is a God who is on the field with His sleeves rolled up. God is involved.

Moses' talk is reaching a climax as we pick it up at the beginning of chapter 4.

FINDING TRUTH

1. Read Deuteronomy 4. Record the following information that the passage gives us:

   i. Moses' major commands to Israel

   ii. Special characteristics of Israel's God

   iii. Special privileges Israel has

This chapter tells us a great deal about how Israel's God differs from other gods and religions. Strangely enough, we can best understand these differences by looking at the chapter back-to-front, starting at verse 32.

Reread Deuteronomy 4:32-40.

2. What key phrases are repeated in verses 35 and 39? What do these phrases mean?

The One and Only

We have reached the grand finale of Moses' first sermon. Having for three chapters reminded Israel of its past, Moses proclaims: "The LORD is God; besides him there is no other" (4:35).

Whenever we read "LORD" in capital letters in the Old Testament, it is representing the *personal name* of God: Yahweh. That is the name God used to introduce Himself to Moses at the burning bush (Ex. 3). It is the personal name of God that the Jews came to consider so holy that they would never write it down or even pronounce it.

With that extra information, consider the significance of Moses' statement in 4:35. In a world where every nation had its own religion and there seemed to be a different idol on every hilltop, Israel's personal God, Yahweh, was *the* God. Other gods don't exist. They are a figment of the imagination. Yahweh created the heavens and the earth. Yahweh put the stars and the moon in their places. Yahweh formed every living thing on this planet. It is this God, Yahweh, who has been getting involved with Israel.

Israel is dealing with the one and only Ruler of the universe!

This is a great lesson. Indeed, this is more than the main point of Moses' first sermon: It is also the fundamental lesson of the entire book of Deuteronomy. Everything else in the whole book flows out of the truth that Yahweh alone is God. It is not until Israel gets that perspective that they will be able to treat Yahweh in the appropriate way.

FINDING TRUTH

Now reread 4:15-24.

1. In light of 4:35 (i.e., that Yahweh alone is God), why are these commands important?

2. From the passage, what are some of the major differences between idols and Yahweh?

Therefore No Idolatry

The above investigation introduces Deuteronomy's strongly emphasized message that idolatry is stupid and worthy of severe punishment. In light of 4:35, it is silly to worship anything that is not God.

To prevent idolatry, Deuteronomy goes further than simply banning the worship of other gods. It also prohibits the worship of images or representations of Yahweh Himself (4:15-18). This is important, because an image of God cannot possibly represent the glory of the one and only God who created all things. How could a created thing be a proper representation of its Creator? It will always be but a pale and distorted image of the truth. An image will mislead you. It will lower the horizons of your understanding of what God is like. The inadequacy of that image will corrupt your appreciation of what God is like.

Yahweh is God; there is no other: therefore, no idolatry, no other gods, and no false images!

But all this raises a major difficulty for Israel. If God doesn't have a form with which we can represent Him, then where does our impression of God come from? What do we have to shape our thinking about Yahweh?

The preceding verses of chapter 4 give us the answer.

FINDING TRUTH

Reread Deuteronomy 4:10-12

1. List the actions the LORD takes at Horeb.

2. Why do you think verse 12 stresses the fact that the LORD was heard but not seen?

God Is Not Dumb

The people of Israel are not to use images of Yahweh, because they have a far better way of knowing and worshiping Him. They have His *words*. It is by remembering His words that Israel will come to revere Yahweh alone as God.

However, Moses makes an even greater claim for Israel. In verse 11 he says, "*You* came near and stood at the foot of the mountain." That's not strictly true, of course. The Israelites whom Moses is addressing here were not at Horeb when God gave the commandments. Remember, this sermon is being given forty years after Horeb. The generation that had gathered at the mountain is now dead (see

1:35). Yet as Moses recounts God's words, he talks to this present generation as though they had been there.

The point is that as they remember Yahweh's words, they share in the experience of God's revelation at Horeb. By the remembrance of God's words, a past encounter with God is passed on from generation to generation. God acts in history, and future generations can share in that experience by hearing God's word.

For this reason, throughout Deuteronomy there is incredible emphasis on the Law and commandments. The Israelites are told to teach the commandments to their children, to talk about them on the way to work, even to write them on the walls of their houses (Deut. 6:6-9). And it's all because these are Yahweh's words.

Yahweh didn't physically appear at Sinai, but He did speak. By remembering what He said, Israel can gain an accurate understanding of what God is like, and they can share in the past actions of God in the history of His people.

This has implications for us. Our God speaks, and we have His words in the Scriptures. If we want to know what God is like, we mustn't rely on images or idols of any type. When we read the Bible we let God speak for Himself!

GOING FURTHER

1. What are some of the popular "images and idols" people use to try to get an impression of what God is like?

From the ideas we have just discussed, how can we evaluate these ways of trying to know God?

2. What implications does this have for what we do in our "quiet time" and at church?

3. Is it difficult to believe that we can know God accurately and fully through His Word? Why or why not?

Deuteronomy and Jesus

We can't leave Moses' first sermon without saying something about Jesus. For one of the great things about the Old Testament is that it shows us the way God does things. And because God is consistent in the way He does things, we can expect to find parallels between God's actions in the Old Testament and His ultimate action in Jesus.

A book like Deuteronomy can help us better understand Jesus by giving us a deeper grasp of His greatness. For example, Deuteronomy has reminded us that Yahweh is the one and only God. That is something we should think through when we consider Jesus. We can fall into the trap of misunderstanding Jesus' servanthood as a kind of weakness—something that means He is easily manipulated. We would never actually say it, but subconsciously we can treat Jesus as a kind of spiritual errand boy.

But when Jesus appeared on this earth He came with all the authority of the Creator of this earth. Jesus walked out into a raging storm, told it to stop—and it did! Jesus told corpses to come back to life—and they did! Jesus walked up to people and said that He was so important that they had to leave everything and follow Him—and they did!

Jesus came as the Boss. You don't tell Jesus what to do. He tells you what to do. We need to remember whom it is we're dealing with.

GOING FURTHER

What factors in your life make it hard to remember that it is Yahweh, the Creator and Boss, with whom you are dealing?

A Gracious God

Proposals

Traditionally February 29, which occurs only in a leap year, is the day when a woman may ask a man to marry her. But the tradition isn't much followed these days; usually a man is supposed to take the romantic lead in proposing to his beloved.

Other types of relationships have stricter rules about who takes the initiative in proposing such a "contract." A boss promises a job to a nervous interviewee. A couple agrees to care for an orphan. The way in which the contract is made, and who takes the first step, tells us a lot about the way the two parties relate to each other.

This study looks at initiatives. In Deuteronomy 5, Moses launches into his second sermon. This sermon is by far the longest in Deuteronomy. It stretches all the way from chapter 5 through chapter 28. Although it is long, the sermon has a simple structure: After telling us more about Yahweh, Moses focuses on how Israel should respond to Him. Moses is still working on the principle that you need to know whom you're dealing with before you can behave appropriately. Moses has already told Israel the most important aspect about God: They are dealing with Yahweh, the one and only God. But there is still more to be said. In this study we will examine one other important attribute of God and His relationship with Israel: God takes the first step.

FINDING TRUTH

Read the start of Moses' second sermon, in Deuteronomy 5:1-32.

1. From this passage, list the initiatives God has taken.

2. What are the terms of the contract between God and Israel? Write a sentence to summarize them.

3. The Ten Commandments can seem like just a list of "dos and don'ts." How does it change our view of them when we know that they are part of God's covenant with Israel?

The Divine Initiative

As Moses starts his second sermon, he introduces Israel to the fact that it was Yahweh who first initiated a relationship with Israel. In Deuteronomy 5:2, Moses speaks of the LORD making a covenant with them. The word *covenant* is like our word *contract*: It's an agreement drawn up between two parties. Moses stresses that it is Yahweh who made the first move in drawing up the contract. Israel didn't go looking for God—God came looking for them.

But how did God do that? What was the first move God made? Moses describes one particularly important event in Deuteronomy 5:6—Israel's escape from Egypt (often called the "Exodus").

In the Exodus, God brought the nation Israel out of slavery in Egypt. (If you're unfamiliar with this event you can read about it in Exodus 1–15.) In a massive show of power, God saved Israel from slavery and thus initiated a relationship with the nation.

But hold on! Didn't God initiate a relationship with Israel prior to the Exodus in His promises to Abraham (Genesis 12, 15; see study

1)? Yes, and He dealt with Jacob and his entire family when He brought them down to Egypt, and later when He rescued them from Egypt in the Exodus. Now, at Mount Sinai, however, God is making this more explicit contract with all of Abraham's descendants at one time—now that they have become a great nation in fulfillment of God's promise.

This point is critical if we are going to properly understand all the different commandments recorded in Deuteronomy, including the Ten Commandments. The Ten Commandments did not *start* Israel's relationship with God. The Ten Commandments gave expression to a relationship that was *already in existence*. In other words, keeping the Ten Commandments is not what saved Israel. They were already saved! God had already brought them out of slavery.

This is important because it can be a point of confusion. Many people think that both we and Israel *earn* our salvation by doing good things. They think that it's up to *us* to start the friendship with God by keeping the Ten Commandments or going to church or having quiet times.

However, the truth is actually the reverse. We humans resist friendship with God; yet He persists in taking the initiative to bring us into a relationship with Him. The only reason we can be friends with God is because He makes the first move. This is an amazing discovery: We cannot propose friendship with God; we can only respond to His offer of friendship. We will consider the implications of this a little later in the study. Let's now turn to consider *why* God bothered to make that first move.

FINDING TRUTH

Read Deuteronomy 7:6-9.

1. Why *didn't* God choose Israel?

2. Why *did* God choose Israel? What was His motivation?

3. Consider the following New Testament passages.

	How did God save us?	Why did God save us?
Romans 5:6-8		
Ephesians 2:8-10		
1 John 4:7-10		

Deuteronomy and Jesus

In this study we have discovered a wonderful thing about our God. He loves people even though they don't deserve it! And the God who loved Israel is the same God who loves us.

Jesus didn't die for us because we're particularly attractive people. On the surface, we might seem all right because we hide our darker side so that other people will like us. But God sees below the surface. God sees all our impure motives and selfish thoughts and fantasies. Yet despite our unattractiveness, God makes the first move to start a friendship with us, as He did with Israel.

While we were powerless and trapped in our sinful little worlds, God sent His own dear Son to die for us. Through Jesus' death, God performed a "second Exodus," rescuing us from slavery to sin. In our sinfulness, we weren't interested in Him—but He was interested in us. While we were still sinners, Christ died for us.

GOING FURTHER

1. Considering how God has acted toward us, how do you think we should respond? Why is our response to God often less than it should be?

2. Why do Christians do good works?

3. If we are to be like God, what has this study shown us about the way we should act toward each other?

When is it difficult to be the one who initiates peace?

4. Imagine that a friend says to you: "Being a Christian is okay for you; you're religious. But if you knew some of the things I've done, you'd know that I'm too bad for God to be interested in me. I'll never change." What would you reply?

A Grateful People

So far, Deuteronomy has painted a very impressive picture of God. We've seen that Yahweh is the one and only God. He is the unique Creator of the world who alone has the right to tell us what to do. We have also seen that God is personal, that He gets involved with His creation, and that He has generously initiated a contract with Israel so as to make them His people.

As Moses' second sermon progresses, however, the focus of Deuteronomy begins to change. The spotlight now starts to fall, not on God, but on Israel.

Now, in some ways this division is a bit artificial. Really, ever since chapter 1 Moses has been explaining to the Israelites various things they ought to be doing for God. Nevertheless, in Deuteronomy 5–6 a shift in focus develops. No longer is most attention given to what God has done for Israel. Now most attention is on what Israel should do for God.

FINDING TRUTH

Read Deuteronomy 6, listing all the different ways in which Israel is to respond to God.

Israel's Response

Chapter 6 is a pivotal chapter in Deuteronomy. In these verses, Moses points out that there is really just one fundamental response that Israel should make to Yahweh. The basic attitude that should undergird all of Israel's behavior is a *love for God.*

This response of love toward God is best summarized in verses 4 and 5. These two verses are known as the *Shema* (which means "Hear!"). Even today, diligent Jews recite these verses as a daily prayer. The *Shema* is significant because it details the fundamental character of God, and then it describes what mankind's fundamental response to God should be.

The Hebrew of verse 4 is a bit ambiguous. It is probably best translated: "Yahweh our God is one Yahweh." There is no other God. Yahweh is the one and only God. He is unique.

This is what we discovered in study 2, at the climax of Moses' first sermon: "Yahweh is God; besides him there is no other" (4:35). Here again in the *Shema*, the idea is repeated as the single most important thing about Yahweh.

And what is our response to this unique God? Verse 5 tells Israel that their fundamental response to God is to love Him with every fiber of their being. Everything they do should flow from a love for God.

GOING FURTHER

1. In what ways do we use the word *love*?

2. What do you think it means to love God?

3. How is it difficult to love God with all our heart, soul, and strength?

But What Is Love?

Love is a funny word. We use it in a wide range of ways. Love can mean different things to different people. I love McDonalds. I love certain types of music. I love my wife. These (hopefully) express different ideas.

In the Bible, love always takes its meaning from the way God has loved us. And how does God love? God loves His people by being committed to them through thick and thin. Irrespective of how stubborn and obnoxious Israel became, God stuck with them. God certainly disciplined them, but only to help them wake up to themselves. God never stopped wanting what was best for Israel. That is biblical love. It is essentially a commitment. Love is not just a warm, fuzzy feeling, although that may be part of it. Love is primarily a deliberate expression of loyalty.

Did you notice the extent of the love Israel was to have for God? It was to be with all their heart, soul, and strength. Half-hearted love is not appropriate. A lukewarm love isn't enough. God deserves more. God's love is all-encompassing, and so His people's response ought to be all-inclusive.

That is how Israel is to live toward God. In Deuteronomy 6, Israel is told to set their loyalty firmly on God. This does make sense. After all, Yahweh *is* God alone. Israel's loyalty should be fixed on Him because nothing else exists that deserves their loyalty. Yahweh is God. Besides Him there is nothing and no one else worth following.

In other words, our love of God must flow into every area of our lives. It's no use declaring our loyalty to God at church, then leaving it behind when we go home. That would show that we don't really appreciate who God is. We need to love God and show our loyalty to Him in every move we make.

The trouble is, we aren't all that good at loving God. What can we do to motivate ourselves? In this regard, Moses gives Israel some invaluable advice.

FINDING TRUTH

Look up the following passages. In each paragraph, what does Moses tell Israel to do? How would this have helped Israel to love God?

- Deuteronomy 6:10-12

- Deuteronomy 6:20-23

- Deuteronomy 7:7-11

The Human Motivation

Israel

Moses tells Israel to remember the past. He urges them to think back to what God has done for them because, as they do so, their love for God will well up into gratitude.

In particular, Moses tells Israel to keep remembering the Exodus. Remember from study 3 that the Exodus was when God made the first move to gather Israel together into one nation. This is what Moses wants the Israelites to tell their children. They should pass the word on, and fix it in their minds, that Yahweh, the God of all creation, has made Israel His own treasured possession. Out of all the peoples of the world, God chose them!

As Israel dwelt on God's love for them, that would prompt them to love Him in return—not in a dry, legalistic way, but in a deep, personal way. Israel's love would flow forth as an expression of gratitude for all that God had done for them.

Deuteronomy and Jesus

Against the backdrop of the Exodus and the awaiting Promised Land, Moses tells Israel that the appropriate response to a God like that is to love Him back. You love Him back with all your heart and soul and strength.

If you're a Christian, the same is true for you. The God of all the universe has made you His child. He has ushered you into heaven for free. Through Jesus, you have been saved from a miserable existence in hell, and the appropriate response to a God who does that for you is surely to love Him back.

Furthermore, remember that Moses warned Israel never to forget their salvation. He told them never to forget the Exodus—the way God made the first move to save them.

The parallel for us is that we must never forget the death of Jesus on the Cross, for that is *the* event which displays beyond question the incredible depths of God's love for us. It was at the Cross that we were saved. It was at the Cross that God took the initiative to enable us to become His people. We must keep the Cross at the center of our faith.

Just as Moses continually called Israel to remember their salvation in the Exodus and to keep it central, we also ought continually to remember our salvation through Jesus' death on the Cross on our behalf. We are to keep it central.

GOING FURTHER

1. What are some of the things that tend to push the Cross out of the center of our lives? How can we stop this from happening? Be specific in your answers.

2. God instructed Israel to love Him with every fiber of their being. What will this involve in our day-to-day lives? (Look at John 15:9-17; 1 John 4:19–5:4.)

3. Deuteronomy 6:6 urges Israel to keep the words Moses is teaching them "upon your hearts." In its ancient Jewish context, this probably refers to memorizing and repeating them. Why not choose a passage (or two) that will remind you of God's generosity to you in Jesus, and commit it to memory!

Love and Trust

Talk Is Cheap

Actions speak louder than words. It's one thing to say something; it's altogether another thing to do it. Talk is cheap. That principle is the dominant thought that now begins to emerge from Deuteronomy.

So far in Deuteronomy we've seen that Israel's God, Yahweh, is the one and only God. We've seen that Yahweh is a generous God who saved Israel from slavery in Egypt, and that Israel's fundamental response to Yahweh should therefore be one of grateful love.

When we come to be practical about loving God, it can be hard to know what it means (you might have found this difficulty during the last study). How do you act out a love for God? What actions show that you love God? This topic dominates the remainder of Moses' second sermon as he spells out the behavior that demonstrates a love for Yahweh. Here we deal with the theme of love and trust; the next study will look at love and obedience.

FINDING TRUTH

Read Deuteronomy 9:23-24.

1. What event do these verses describe?

2. What two things characterized Israel's rebellion against God?

Love = Trust + Obedience

Israel's first attempt to gain the Promised Land ended in disaster because Israel rebelled against God's command to enter and conquer the land. As punishment, God caused Israel to wander in the desert for forty years. Moses describes Israel's rebellion as a lack of *trust* and *obedience*. Despite the great salvation from Egypt that God had performed for them, they failed to trust and obey Him.

Deuteronomy provides a great deal of instruction about how Israel's experience of wandering in the wilderness should have taught them the importance of trust and obedience.

FINDING TRUTH

Read Deuteronomy 8.

1. What was the lesson of the manna?

2. What were the implications of this lesson for Israel's future?

The Lesson of the Manna

While in the wilderness, every morning the Israelites had to go out and gather just the right amount of manna to feed themselves for the day. They weren't allowed to gather a surplus and store it up for the future. When some of them did try that, the manna went bad overnight. When they awoke it was full of maggots. The only exception to the rule was on the sixth day, when the people were to gather twice as much manna so that they could rest the next day—the Sabbath. Whenever the people did that, the manna did not go bad overnight. (Exodus 16 tells the whole story.)

In Deuteronomy 8, Moses tells Israel that the manna experience was designed to humble them and force them to trust Yahweh. Each morning when they awoke, Israel had to trust that God had not forgotten them. Every single day they had to trust Yahweh to feed them, and not once did He fail them (v. 4). The purpose of the manna was to show Israel that when they came to the edge of the Promised Land the second time around, this time they were to trust God (v. 5).

The manna experience also had implications for Israel's future. In the luxury of the Promised Land, they were not to forget that everything comes from God (vv. 10, 16-18). They were not to fall into the trap of thinking that this life of ease had come to them because of their own skills. They were to remember that it came from God. Trust in God was to characterize Israel's ongoing life in the Promised Land.

FINDING TRUTH

Read quickly through the laws mentioned in Deuteronomy 14–15. In what ways do you think these laws foster trust in God?

Whom Do You Trust?

In this study, we are seeing again the way God deals with people and the way God's people ought to respond to Him. Israel had experienced a wonderful salvation, and in grateful response they were called upon to love God and to express that love by trusting Him.

We're not all that different. The only real difference is that we have experienced an even more wonderful salvation. Through Jesus' death on the Cross, God has saved us from hell, and as His people He calls on us to love Him and to express that love in terms of trust.

First and foremost, we are to trust God for our salvation. God has promised us that, because of what Jesus achieved on the Cross, we have forgiveness for our sins. He tells us to trust that promise.

Often, however, our trust in God doesn't really spill over into our daily lives. That is especially the case when God's perspective doesn't agree with ours, and that's exactly why Israel had failed in their first attempt to enter the Promised Land. God's perspective was, "Don't worry, I'll help you." Israel's perspective was, "No way! The Canaanites are too strong for us!" Israel trusted their own opinion more than God's. They refused to love and trust Him.

We need to learn from Israel's mistakes.

GOING FURTHER

1. Do you feel that God makes unreasonable demands upon our trust? In what areas is it difficult to trust Him?

Do you trust God's advice even if you think He's wrong?

2. Tom is a regular churchgoer who has a healthy respect for God's judgment and a correct hatred for sin in his own life. Every night he thinks back over the day to remember all of his sins and ask for forgiveness for each of them. He wants to make himself pure in God's sight, so he doesn't go to sleep until he knows that he has covered every sin of the day. Is Tom trusting God? Why or why not?

3. Write down whether the following statements are true or false, and why.

   a. To totally trust God, I have to "let go" of myself.

   b. It is wrong to plan for the future; we should just trust God.

c. If we trust God, things will always work out well.

d. Trust is chiefly an attitude of the mind.

Love and Obedience

In Australia we have a health food product called Vegemite, and at our home we keep it in the fridge, even though I think that's a funny place to put it. It actually never crossed my mind to keep Vegemite in the fridge before I met my wife, Sue. As I was growing up, my family used to keep it in the cupboard. Nowadays, I put the Vegemite in the fridge, because that's where Sue used to keep it with her family. Sue likes the Vegemite to be in the fridge and now so do I.

You will no doubt be wondering just how Vegemite and Deuteronomy can occur in the same paragraph. The point is that love and obedience are very closely linked. I don't put the Vegemite in the fridge because there's a big sign on the door declaring, "Thou shalt put the Vegemite in the fridge" (there isn't). I do it because I love my wife; I like to make her happy. My love for her results in my doing what pleases her.

In Deuteronomy, Moses applies this same lesson to Israel. Remember from study 4 that Israel is meant to love Yahweh out of thankfulness for all that He has done for them. That love is meant to be shown through Israel's trust in God (study 5). Now Moses goes on to explain that Israel's love for God should also express itself through *obedience* to Him.

FINDING TRUTH

Read Deuteronomy 11.

1. In what ways are love and obedience linked in this chapter? Look particularly at verses 1, 13, and 22.

2. What should Israel's past experiences have taught them about obedience? (vv. 1-7)

3. What will happen to Israel if they obey God?

4. What will be the consequences of disobedience?

Learning from the Wilderness

In our last study, we learned that the experience with the manna in the wilderness should have shown Israel that they can *trust* God. Indeed, if in the future they fail to trust Yahweh, they will get themselves into deep trouble (8:19-20).

In Deuteronomy 11 Moses emphasizes that, in the same way, Israel should *obey* God. The chapter opens with the story of Dathan and Abiram, who had disobeyed God in the desert and paid the penalty. They treated Yahweh with contempt, complaining about Moses' leadership and being ungrateful for God's provision in the wilderness. They broke their covenant with God, and as punishment the earth literally swallowed them up. (The whole story is in Numbers 16:1-35.)

God reminds Israel of such events to show them that obeying Him is important. If they don't obey God, discipline and punishment will follow.

This is an important lesson because it has implications for the future, as the rest of the chapter spells out. Once Israel has entered the Promised Land, if they obey God they will be blessed. They will receive good harvests and plenty of rain, and the land will flow with milk and honey. Obedience will bring blessing. Disobedience, however, will bring God's curse. Crops will fail. There will be famine and drought and, if Israel still doesn't wake up, God will kick them out of the Promised Land altogether. Obedience will bring blessing. Disobedience will bring curses.

In the rest of his second sermon, right up to the end of chapter 26, Moses goes on to describe a lot of specific ways in which Israel is to obey God once they enter the Promised Land. For most people, this is where the reading gets tough. There are lots and lots of laws—and strange ones, like the one about the bird's nest. Let's look at these laws now and see if we can understand their place in the message of Deuteronomy. (You will probably need to skim-read to get through these chapters.)

Four Important Themes

If we look, one by one, at the laws in chapters 12–26, we will get not only exhausted but also confused and possibly even despondent. Why are they so detailed? Why do they often refer to strange practices and customs that we know nothing about? Does God intend for us to follow these laws?

The verse-by-verse approach may not be the most helpful here. If we try to look at the laws given as a package, we should be able to make more sense of them. Many of the laws can be grouped under four major themes. We'll discuss these as we go.

Theme 1: The Exhaustive Nature of Obedience.

A huge range of topics is covered under the laws in these chapters. The point being made is that all of life comes under God's dominion. The laws don't cover every possible life situation, but by their breadth and their diversity they show that no area of life is irrelevant to God. Nothing is untouched by His requirement of obedience.

FINDING TRUTH

1. Quickly read Deuteronomy 21–23 and list all the general areas of life that are mentioned.

2. From your understanding of Deuteronomy so far, why do you think the Law is so broad in scope? (See Deut. 6:5.)

Theme 2: Laws That Extend the Ten Commandments

Many of the laws are extensions of the Ten Commandments, showing how the principles of the Ten Commandments apply to life in the Promised Land. The Ten Commandments were originally given at Mt. Sinai in the wilderness, but they were to have ongoing importance in shaping Israel's life in Canaan.

FINDING TRUTH

Read Deuteronomy 16:18–17:7 and reread Deuteronomy 22. Note any laws that are specific applications of the Ten Commandments. (You might not fill every box.)

COMMANDMENT	EXTENSION
Have no other gods.	
Have no idols.	
Do not misuse God's name.	
Remember the Sabbath.	
Honor father and mother.	
Don't murder.	
Don't commit adultery.	
Don't steal.	
Don't give false testimony.	
Don't covet.	

Theme 3: Laws That Remind Israel of God's Holiness

Many laws were a constant reminder of the holiness of God. Observance of the Law meant that every Israelite ate, slept, drank, and moved within a community that constantly hammered home the point that God is holy.

FINDING TRUTH

Reread 23:9-14. How do these laws reinforce that God's holiness should influence every aspect of Israel's life?

Theme 4: Laws That Promote Godliness

Not all the laws can be linked directly back to one of the Ten Commandments. Many of them reflect the truth that Israel was to imitate God in the way they did things. By obeying these laws, Israel was to become more like God.

We need to think carefully at this point. Although these laws encouraged godliness in Israel, that *doesn't* mean that we also must follow these specific instructions. Instead, we need to look behind the specific law and identify the aspect of God that it is drawing on. For example, consider the law about overlooking a sheaf while you are harvesting (24:19). It is a mistake to think that this law prohibits modern combine harvesters, which don't leave any sheaves. We can't simply apply the Old Testament laws to ourselves like that, because we live in a different age—and I don't mean the twentieth century: We live in the age of the New Covenant, the age after Christ.

In this age, Christians are no longer under the Law (see, e.g., Rom. 6:14). The laws Moses gave to Israel describe behavior for the Old Covenant, not the New. They still have relevance for us as examples of what pleases God, and as warnings of what happens to the disobedient, but they do not apply to us directly (see Rom. 15:4; 1 Cor. 10:6, 11). Someone has described the Old Testament laws as being like a retired professor: He is very useful to go to for advice, but he no longer gives exams.

What we should do is look behind the Law to consider the aspect of God's character to which it is referring. In the case of Deuteronomy 24:19, it is that God is merciful and that He looks after the needy (see also Deut. 10:18-19). If we are to be godly, we should also be merciful and look after the needy.

FINDING TRUTH

Read the laws given in Deuteronomy 13.

1. What characteristics of God do these laws draw upon?

2. How should these characteristics of God shape our lives today?

Obeying Jesus

The four themes above provide a general overview of the specific laws God gave to Israel, laws that were to motivate Israel to be holy in every area of life by reminding them that they were constantly in the presence of a holy God.

We must be careful, however, that while in the maze of all these specific commandments we don't forget the motivation behind them all. It's easy to misunderstand all these laws as being heavy-handed and oppressive. Remember that Israel was to obey God out of love. Israel wasn't to keep all these laws out of dry, sterile legalism. They were to be kept as a labor of love.

In the same way, we should obey God out of our love for Him. If we are Christians, then God has graciously saved us. God has brought us out of the bondage of sin and death through the death and resurrection of Jesus. God has made us His people, and in response to that we ought to love Him with thankful hearts. And just like Israel, our love should show itself in obedience. Jesus said, "If you love me you will obey what I command" (John 14:15).

GOING FURTHER

1. Do you try to obey God out of love for Him?

Read 1 John 5:1-5.

2. Does obedience to God seem burdensome?

Why should it not be burdensome?

The Leader We Had to Lose

As we reach Moses' third and final sermon in Deuteronomy (Deut. 29–33), the unimaginable is about to happen. Moses is about to die.

For Israel, Moses' death would have been almost impossible to comprehend. Moses *was* Israel. To them it might have seemed that the nation existed only because of Moses. Moses had been on the scene ever since the Exodus, and the political, religious, economic, and social structures of Israel all depended on him. The thought of being without Moses was surely very frightening.

But the unimaginable is about to happen, so the daunting question that must be faced is: "What now? How do we replace someone like Moses?"

In one sense, they couldn't replace Moses. Indeed, the book ends by saying just that (34:10-12). Israel would never get another Moses. He was unique.

But life must go on. Israel can't just fade away because Moses isn't around anymore. A replacement has to be found. Alternative strategies that don't depend on Moses have to be put in place, and that is precisely what happens in these last few chapters. Like any good leader, before he dies Moses tries to make himself redundant. He puts in place people and structures to ensure that Israel will continue.

In this study we will examine three main things that Moses plans for Israel's future.

FINDING TRUTH

Read Deuteronomy 31:1-8.

1. After mentioning his own death, what is the first thing Moses tells Israel? (vv. 3-6)

2. How would this have been an encouragement for Israel?

3. What other thing does Moses organize for Israel's future? (Look also at 31:23.)

Why was this a wise thing to do even though Moses wasn't dead yet?

A New Leader

One of Moses' first plans for the future was to designate his replacement. Israel had known for quite a while that Joshua would be its leader (see Num. 27:12-22), but it is now, with Moses on his deathbed, that Joshua gets the official endorsement.

It must have been greatly reassuring to Joshua to receive God's word of encouragement in Deuteronomy 31:23. No doubt he would have been feeling nervous about filling Moses' shoes, but God promises that just as He helped Moses, so He will help Joshua. Joshua is to find comfort in the fact that God keeps His word.

FINDING TRUTH

Read Deuteronomy 31:9-13.

1. What plan for Israel's future does Moses put in place?

2. Why is this plan so important? (You might like to refer back to the section "God Is Not Dumb" in study 2.)

A New Mediator

Moses was more than just a political leader. Moses was also a mediator between God and Israel. God would talk to Moses, and Moses would pass the message on to the rest of Israel. He brought the word of God to them.

However, after Moses' death, this arrangement will change. The way in which Israel receives God's word will be different. Moses the mediator is to be replaced by the Law. Everything God has told Moses is to be written down and read out in full, every seven years, before all the nation. Through the reading of the Law, God will again address the nation.

This tells us something about the permanence of God's word. Once God has said something, it stays said. When God speaks, He says profound things of ongoing relevance. So the Law is to be read and reread by Israel.

GOING FURTHER

1. Do we consider God's Word this highly?

2. Why is God's Word as relevant today as it was when it was first given?

A Choice to Make

Moses' third step in preparation for his death is to put pressure on Israel to make up their mind once and for all whether or not they intend to follow God when they enter the Promised Land. He calls on them to stop procrastinating and finally to make a decision one way or the other.

FINDING TRUTH

Read Deuteronomy 30:11-20.

1. What are the choices for Israel?

2. How is each choice made?

3. What are the consequences of each choice?

4. What does it mean to say that this choice is "not too difficult for you or beyond your reach"? (vv. 11-14)

The decision Israel has to make is between life or death. It's the choice between God's way and their own way. God's way will bring blessing, and 30:16-19 is full of allusions back to God's promises to Abraham in Genesis 12 (see study 1). In Genesis 12, God promised that Abraham's descendants would increase and be numerous, that Yahweh would bless them and that they would have a land to live in.

Now Israel faces a moment of decision. Yahweh has already begun to fulfil His promises to Abraham, but now is the time for national response.

If they love God and follow in His ways, they will live life to the full. They will live life the way the Creator intended it to be lived. They will enjoy all that God has to offer in His promises to mankind: God's people in God's land being blessed by God. It will be like the Garden of Eden all over again, full of pleasure and joy.

The alternative is a life full of curses. Disobedience to God will lead to Israel's being cut off from God's plan. They will face destruction rather than prosperity, and they will be torn out of the Promised Land. (Read Deuteronomy 28 for a graphic description of these alternatives.)

Obedience to God will bring a life of joy. Rejecting God will bring a life of curses. The choice Moses is putting before Israel is no light matter. Moses closes this portion of his address, highlighting the seriousness of the decision by calling heaven and earth as witnesses (30:19).

GOING FURTHER

1. Do we take God's call to obedience seriously? Do we see it as a matter of life and death?

2. The choice for Israel seems so obvious. Why is it that so many people don't want to follow God's way?

Jesus: The Future of Israel

We have been considering the future plans that Moses put in place. God's ultimate future plan for Israel was Jesus. Israel wasn't left in the dark about this plan, even at this stage. It was clear to the Israelites who were about to enter the Promised Land that a leader greater than Moses was yet to come.

In Deuteronomy 18:15-22, God promised that He would send prophets to Israel to tell them His word. As the Old Testament period came to an end, these verses were understood in an increasingly specific way. People began looking for a single, special prophet who would be as great as Moses (see John 1:21).

Jesus stepped into history as the Prophet predicted in Deuteronomy 18. Acts 3:11-26 confirms this, as Peter explains that the time of which Moses spoke has now come. In great excitement, we are told that the promises God made to Abraham way back in Genesis have now reached fulfillment in Jesus Christ. The great Leader has come:

> *"Indeed, all the prophets from Samuel on, as many as have spoken, have foretold these days. And you are heirs of the prophets and of the covenant God made with your fathers. He said to Abraham, 'Through your offspring all peoples on earth will be blessed.' When God raised up his servant, he sent him first to you to bless you by turning each of you from your wicked ways."*
>
> —Acts 3:24-25

GOING FURTHER

Read Deuteronomy 18:15-22.

Now read Hebrews 1:1-4 and John 1:14-18.

1. How is Jesus a greater prophet than Moses?

2. What is the word that Jesus came to speak?

Happily Ever After?

People pay a lot of attention to a dying person's last words. We expect that on their deathbeds people will speak their minds. Some will have hope, some despair. Either way, they will probably tell us what they really think.

Israel must have wondered what Moses' final message to them would be. What would God say for the last time through the mouth of Moses? Would He predict that they are to live happily ever after, secure in the land of prosperity and pleasure?

The stage seems set for such a joyous and triumphant conclusion. Moses will die, but Israel seems set to succeed. Now Moses delivers God's final words to them, in the form of a song. After hearing God's commands and His offer of life, Israel might have been unpleasantly surprised by what they heard.

FINDING TRUTH

Read Deuteronomy 31:14-22.

1. What do these verses predict about:

   - how Israel will respond to God?

   - how God will respond to Israel?

2. God dictated to Moses a song about Israel's behavior (see 31:19). Read the first part of this song in Deuteronomy 32:1-20.

   ▲ What do these verses say about God?

   ▲ What do they say about Israel?

3. How would you describe the mood at the end of Deuteronomy?

The Prospect of Failure

If there is one thing that comes through in the final chapters of Deuteronomy, it is the insistence that Israel is again going to mess up its relationship with God. The whole of the wilderness experience was meant to discipline the Israelites for their past rebellion. Yet here we find evidence that they have not learned from their mistakes.

In study 7, we saw that Moses urged the Israelites to make up their minds and to choose God's way once and for all. Deuteronomy 31–32 shows us Israel's answer. God looks into the future and sees that Israel will again choose not to follow Him.

Sadly, Israel's history reveals that this is exactly what happened. Despite the forty years of discipline in the wilderness, when Israel finally entered the Promised Land they fell in a heap. There were civil wars, corrupt kings, and widespread idolatry, and finally Yahweh tore Israel out of His Promised Land by sending Assyria and then Babylon to conquer them. You can read all about it in 1 and 2 Kings.

But back here in Deuteronomy, God has already predicted it. And so the book closes on a note of distress. Deuteronomy began full of hope. God's people were on the edge of entering God's land. Certainly they had made some mistakes in the past—but they'd had forty years in the desert to think about it. Like a father with his son, God had been lovingly, patiently teaching Israel that they could trust Him and that they should obey Him. It was almost as if the Garden of Eden was going to be revisited. God formed Adam and Eve and put them in the garden and blessed them. God again had formed Himself a people, and He was about to put them into His land. If they were obedient, He would bless them.

Deuteronomy starts with such potential and promise, but here at the end, sin again rears its ugly head. If the potential is for the Garden of Eden to be revisited, the reality is that the Fall will also be revisited. Adam and Eve sinned and were removed from the garden. Israel is going to sin and be removed from the Promised Land.

It's all a bit depressing. And deliberately so!

As Deuteronomy closes on this disappointing note, it pushes us to ask the question, What on earth is God going to do about sin? Is there any way at all for God to finally deal with sin?

It is with such questions ringing in our ears that the book of Deuteronomy points us straight to Jesus.

FINDING TRUTH

Read Matthew 4:1-11.

1. What is the possible significance of the location of these events?

2. Compare the devil's temptations of Jesus with the temptations Israel experienced in the wilderness. How are they similar?

How are they different?

3. Look up the quotes with which Jesus answers the devil. Why do you think Jesus responded to the devil by quoting from these passages in Deuteronomy?

4. In what ways is Jesus in Matthew 4 similar to Israel in Deuteronomy?

In what ways is He different?

Jesus: The Solution to Sin

Matthew makes a strong comparison between Jesus and Israel. Israel spent forty years being disciplined in the desert, but they didn't learn. Sin still destroyed their relationship with God. Jesus is tempted for forty days in the desert, but this time no sin is committed. In fact, Jesus quotes the lessons from Deuteronomy that Israel should have learned!

Matthew is telling us something very exciting. Here, now, is someone who is going to succeed where Israel failed. Here is someone who will form a new Israel where sin will be conquered, where people will be free to enter God's Kingdom and enjoy His blessings.

Jesus' trust in and obedience to God reach a pinnacle as He goes to the Cross for our sake. Jesus' death is the punishment we should have received for our failures. Jesus' death, therefore, breaks the grip of sin in our lives and opens the way for God to forgive us and make us His obedient children. Moreover, as followers of Jesus we have such a close relationship with God that His Spirit lives in us, enabling us to put to death our sinful nature.

Deuteronomy prepares us for this wonderful event—the death of Jesus. Deuteronomy describes a time in Israel's history when Israel was on the verge of living the way Yahweh intended for them to live. By gratefully loving Yahweh, by trusting and obeying Him, Israel could have entered the Promised Land and lived life to the full. Yet the predictions were there, even in Deuteronomy, that this would not happen. Human sinfulness would again destroy everything.

Deuteronomy, therefore, describes a time of disappointment, a time that serves to highlight even further the greatness of Jesus. Deuteronomy describes for us the seriousness of sin in order that we might more fully appreciate Christ's sacrifice for us. Israel was still trapped by their sin. Through Jesus' death and resurrection, sin is destroyed. Through Jesus, *we* have the opportunity of a fresh start and a fresh heart.

GOING FURTHER

1. Jesus is God's solution to the problem of evil in the world, but what other solutions do people try to put forward?

2. What practical steps can you take in order to tell people about God's solution to sin?

Read Hebrews 3:12–4:2.

3. What other lessons can we learn from the example of Israel's sin?

What was at the core of their problem?

What can we do to make sure we don't fall into the same trap?

FAITHWALK
BIBLE STUDIES

Notes

Notes

About Matthias Media

This Bible study guide, part of the *FaithWalk Bible Studies,* was originally developed and published in Australia by Matthias Media. Matthias Media is an evangelical publisher focusing on producing resources for Christian ministry. For further information about Matthias Media products, visit their website at: www.matthiasmedia.com.au; or contact them by E-mail at: matmedia@ozemail.com.au; or by fax at: 61-2-9662-4289.